Scandinavian Christmas Crafts

Scandinavian Christmas Crafts

OVER 45 PROJECTS AND QUICK IDEAS FOR BEAUTIFUL DECORATIONS & GIFTS

Christiane Bellstedt Myers

Photography by Caroline Arber

CICO BOOKS

*Dedicated with love to the three men in my life: Neil, Nicholas, and Stefan;
and to my parents Arnulf and Brigitte, who taught me the beauty of the homemade.*

This edition published in 2025 by CICO Books
An imprint of Ryland Peters & Small Ltd
20–21 Jockey's Fields   1452 Davis Bugg Road
London WC1R 4BW   Warrenton, NC 27589
www.rylandpeters.com
Email: euregulations@rylandpeters.com

First published in 2017 as *Scandi Christmas*

10 9 8 7 6 5 4 3 2 1

Text © Christiane Bellstedt Myers 2017, 2025
Design, illustration, and photography © CICO Books 2017, 2025

The designs in this book are copyright and must not be made for sale.

The author's moral rights have been asserted. All rights reserved. No part of this publication may be reproduced, stored in a retrieval system, or transmitted in any form or by any means, electronic, mechanical, photocopying, or otherwise, without the prior permission of the publisher.

A CIP record for this book is available from the British Library. US Library of Congress CIP data has been applied for.

ISBN: 978-1-80065-426-6

Printed in China

Editor: Clare Sayer
Designer: Luana Gobbo
Photographer: Caroline Arber
Illustrator: Stephen Dew
Stylists: Sophie Martell and Joanna Thornhill

In-house editor: Anna Galkina
Art director: Sally Powell
Production controller: Mai-Ling Collyer
Publishing manager: Penny Craig
Publisher: Cindy Richards
Head of production: Patricia Harrington

The authorised representative in the EEA is Authorised Rep Compliance Ltd., Ground Floor. 71 Lower Baggot Street, Dublin, D01 P593, Ireland
www.arccompliance.com

SAFETY NOTE: never leave lit candles unattended or within reach of young children

CONTENTS

Introduction 6

CHAPTER ONE
PAPER AND GLITTER 8
Collage Christmas cards and gift tags 10
Quick idea: Wrapped candles 13
Glitter paper trees 14
Quick idea: Glitter star decorations 17
Santa gift tags 18
Music paper angels 20
Advent envelopes 22
Quick idea: Glitter jars 25
Bobbin decorations 26
Danish paper cones 28
Star garland 30
Quick idea: Stamped giftwrap 32
Quick idea: Stamped clothespins 33

CHAPTER TWO
NATURAL CHRISTMAS 34
Crab apple wreath 36
Quick idea: Hyacinth bulbs in a tin 38
Quick idea: Heart pillar candles 39
Little forest advent candle tin 40
Quick idea: Apple tea lights 43
Pine cone family 44
Quick idea: Simple wire wreath 47
Twig tree 48
Quick idea: Anise wreath 51
Pine cone firelighters 52
Quick idea: Ivy garland 54
Quick idea: Twig candle holders 55

CHAPTER THREE
HOMESPUN FABRICS 56
Heart wreath 58
Quick idea: Fabric-covered cans 61
Patchwork quilt baubles 62
Old window frame display 64
Quick idea: Covered matchbox 67
Fabric garland 68
Mistletoe wreath 70
Clove-scented Christmas trees 72
Framed Christmas pictures 74
Tea light apron 76
Mitten garland 78
Hygge wool bag 80
Embroidered hand towels 82
Christmas stockings 84
Quick idea: Jar covers 87
Christmas tree cushion 88
Tomte or Little Nisse 92
Quick idea: Little embroidered decorations 94
Embroidered Christmas napkins 95
Quick idea: Mini stockings 97

CHAPTER FOUR
CINNAMON AND GINGERBREAD 98
Gingerbread hanging decorations 100
Gingerbread house 102
Gingerbread salt dough wreath 106

Hand stitches 108
Templates 112
Suppliers 124
Index 126
Acknowledgments 127

INTRODUCTION

Old-fashioned, handmade, home-baked, and homespun are all words that describe my perfect Christmas. In this modern, hectic but beautiful world of ours sometimes it is nice to take stock of what is important, especially at this special time of year. Setting a calm but magical scene for the festive season using a traditional palette of red and green will evoke memories of Christmases long ago.

I have been very fortunate to have very dear friends who live in Scandinavia. Having visited them at different times of the year, I find that winter wraps me up in that *hygge* feeling that we have all now come to appreciate. Candles seem to fit into every corner. Big fire baskets line the streets while people shop. Fresh greenery decorates every windowsill and doorway, in stores and homes alike. The warm scent of cinnamon fills the air. The twinkle of little white lights glistening everywhere creates a feeling of warmth and welcome and although the temperatures are below freezing, you never feel the cold. The most wonderful thing about Scandinavia is that everyone participates in decorating for the season. It is rare to see a darkened home in the neighborhood. My most endearing memory was passing by an old graveyard where all I saw were flickering lights here and there like fireflies. My friend explained that lanterns replace flowers at gravesides at this time of year. How wonderful that the feeling of light and love extends to those who have shared Christmases past.

The key to creating a Scandinavian Christmas is to keep everything simple. It does help that a lot of Scandinavian homes are decorated in muted shades of white and gray, which makes the red and green of Christmas decorations look even more beautiful. I have tried in this book to create projects that will give your home a touch of Scandinavia. The projects themselves range from very quick and easy to those that will require just a little more time. When you decide to start creating it is best that you gather together all the materials that you will need to complete the project. Nothing stops the flow of making and creating more than having to hunt for something you need before you are finished.

I like to make my workspace as comfortable as possible, which is what I do at meetings of The Cozy Club (workshops where I invite people into my home to make seasonal crafts). It not only adds to the ambience but also encourages creativity. I light tea lights here and there and I make sure that the kettle is ready to go. Christmas carols play softly in the background and a selection of cinnamon-spiced goodies are temptingly laid out. The chair I sit in must be plumped up with pretty pillows and all my materials are ready to be used.

I hope that you will enjoy making these projects as much as I have loved creating them. There was not one day that I did not love what I was doing, from the sewing, baking, and gluing to the writing, editing, styling, and photography days. If this book instills in you the joy of an old-fashioned Scandinavian Christmas and urges you to start making your own Scandi Christmas, then I will be content! I would just love to see what you have made. Now, light those candles, make some tea, and choose a project.

With love from my Christmas house to yours...

Chris xxx

CHAPTER ONE
PAPER AND GLITTER

We all have piles of paper in the recycling box. There is something very satisfying about creating a beautiful decorative item with something that was destined to be thrown away. I can imagine after you have made a few of these projects, you will take a second look at what paper you discard. The magic is simple—just add a touch of glitter. Glitter is really one of my favorite things; I add it to anything that I can. Keep to one or two colors—I prefer to use white or silver at this time of year as it reminds me of glistening snow. Take that pinch of magic and let your creations shimmer.

COLLAGE CHRISTMAS CARDS and GIFT TAGS

In this day of emails and text messages, the simple notion of sending a card through the mail is becoming something of a rarity. When you reuse old cards, letters, and tags, and spend time creating, you are being very eco-friendly! Many friends and family who have received gift tags from me have kept them over the years to decorate their trees, so the tag remains a happy memory and a reminder of many a Christmas past.

MATERIALS

Thick white artist paper or card stock, approximately letter or A4 size

Old cards and tags

Selection of decorative papers, giftwrap, old sheet music, old books, etc.

Glitter

Baker's twine

Small silver jingle bells

Tools

Templates on page 112

Scissors

Small paintbrush

White craft (PVA) glue

Ink pad and stamps

1 Fold the artist paper in half to create a greeting card. Surround yourself with all your papers. Using the templates on page 112, cut out some shapes such as hearts, stars, and trees. The cut-outs can be used on the inside of the card while the shapes left in the paper that you used to cut it out can be filled in with different paper to add more interest.

2 Using craft (PVA) glue, start covering the card with scraps of paper, overlapping them in places and leaving some areas blank so that you can add some Christmas motifs using stamps and an ink pad. When you are happy with your work, add a little glue here and there and sprinkle some glitter for that touch of magic.

3 Finally, take some baker's twine and wrap it around the spine of the card. Thread a small jingle bell onto the twine and tie a knot to secure.

4 To make a gift tag, use the same technique, but this time using a tag that you can tie onto a gift.

QUICK IDEA: WRAPPED CANDLES

Sometimes the simplest things create the biggest impression—this quick project does just that. I do this when I am heading out to an impromptu meal and want to bring a unique gift. I pick a bottle of wine and wrap up some of these candles to tie onto the bottle—and the hostess is always very pleased!

MATERIALS

Long dinner candles
Brown Kraft (parcel) paper
Decorative giftwrap
Small silver jingle bells
String or twine

Tools

Scissors

1 Take three candles and wrap each one with a piece of brown paper. Make sure that the candles are not completely covered.

2 Wrap a smaller piece of decorative giftwrap around all three candles. Tie it all together with string or twine, add a few jingle bells, and you're done.

GLITTER PAPER TREES

There is something special about being able to create a stunning centerpiece for your Christmas table without spending a lot of money. Adding a pinch of glitter reflects the light, making your table shimmer and feel magical and festive. Make a large tree or several smaller ones—or whatever combination works best for you!

MATERIALS

Oasis block

Terra cotta plant pot (I used an antique terra cotta pot but any would work)

Wooden skewers

Paper (preferably old newspaper with a Christmas story or old sheet music)

Silver glitter

Tools

Craft knife

Small paintbrush

White craft (PVA) glue

Star cookie cutter (or use the template on page 115)

Pencil

Clothespin

1 Use a craft knife to cut a piece of oasis from the block. Make sure that the oasis fits into the plant pot snugly. Push a wooden skewer vertically into the center of the oasis, with the pointed end at the top. You may want to trim the wooden skewer, depending on the size of your pot.

2 Take your paper in bunches of three or four pages and rip them into squares of varying sizes. There is no need to be precise; it is actually much cuter when the edges of the paper are not straight.

3. Start pushing your bundles of paper onto the skewer. Turn the pot slightly as you add more paper bundles so that the edges of the paper are not all lined up evenly. You want to gradually decrease the size of the torn squares to resemble the shape of a tree.

4. Take a small paintbrush and use it to spread glue on the edges of the paper. Sprinkle with as much silver glitter as you want! (Do this over a piece of old newspaper so you can catch and reuse the excess glitter.)

5. Use a cookie cutter or one of the templates on page 115 to draw and cut out two star shapes.

6. Apply some glue on one star and press the other star onto it with the tip of the skewer sandwiched in the middle. Use the clothespin to hold the star in place while the glue dries; remove when the glue is dry. Paint the star with a little more glue and sprinkle with glitter to finish.

QUICK IDEA: GLITTER STAR DECORATIONS

MATERIALS
Thick artist paper or card stock
Glitter

Tools
Templates on page 115 (optional)
Scissors
Small paintbrush
White craft (PVA) glue
Needle and invisible thread

Sparkle, shimmer, and glitter are all words that conjure up a magical feeling which is prevalent at Christmas. A very easy, fun, and economical way to add this to your home is by making some glitter stars. Be warned... you will find glitter everywhere long after Christmas, but to me, that only adds to the wonder of the season!

1 Cut out various shapes of stars (you can use the templates on page 115 or cut them freehand) and paint on a thin layer of glue.

2 Sprinkle on some glitter so the stars are totally covered and let them dry. When they are dry, turn them over and add glue and glitter to the other side.

3 After the stars are completely dry, thread your needle and make a hanging loop with invisible thread. Now, let the magic begin!

SANTA GIFT TAGS

It is always lovely to receive a gift that has been lovingly wrapped and then topped with a homemade tag. These ones are pretty enough to add to the tree as a decoration.

MATERIALS

Thick white artist paper or card stock

Red paper

Scrap of patterned paper (or use a contrasting color)

Natural wool roving (or cotton wool)

Mini gift tag (optional)

Tools

Template on page 114

Pencil

Scissors

White craft (PVA) glue

Black marker pen

1 Using the template on page 114, trace and cut out the Santa from thick white artist paper. Repeat to cut out a Santa in red paper. Cut out the small sack shape from the patterned or contrasting paper.

2 Glue the red Santa onto the white Santa and then glue the sack in place. Use the black marker to color the boots black.

3 Pull out a small amount of the wool roving and use your fingers to manipulate it into the right shapes to fit Santa's beard, coat, and hat trim. Glue in place.

4 You can hang your Santa tag by looping some string around his neck or simply sliding him under the ribbon of a present. If you like you can add a mini gift tag to the string around Santa's neck.

MUSIC PAPER ANGELS

A Christmas tree isn't complete unless it has a few angels—with this next design you will want to make lots of them. They are full of personality and can be easily attached to the branches by pushing down on the clothespin.

MATERIALS

Thick white artist paper or card stock
Old sheet music
Old-style wooden clothespins
Glitter
Florist's wire
Silver jingle bells

Tools
Template on page 114
Pencil
Scissors
White craft (PVA) glue

1 Use the template on page 114 to draw and cut out one set of wings from the artist paper and two sets of wings from the sheet music.

2 Glue the music sheet wings onto both sides of the artist paper wings. Add some glue to the clothespin and press the wings and the clothespin together; let the glue dry. Add some glue to the wings and sprinkle with glitter.

3 Cut a piece of florist's wire about 8 in. (20 cm) long and wrap around the "neck" of the clothespin, leaving two ends like arms. Wrap each end tightly around a pencil a few times. Pull the pencil out and arrange the wire to suit you. Add a little bell to one of the "hands." Draw little eyes with your pencil.

ADVENT ENVELOPES

The excitement of Christmas begins on December first when the Advent calendars are put out. It is fun to find different ways to carry on this tradition; with this project you not only have the calendar, but also a very sweet decorative item. It is very exciting to see a lovely old trug filled to the brim with tempting-looking packages, sealed until their own special day allows them to be opened.

MATERIALS

Roll of brown Kraft (parcel) paper (or enough to make 24 envelopes)

Selection of giftwrap, old sheet music, old Christmas cards, etc.

Matt varnish (such as Mod Podge®)

Small gifts or candies to fill the envelopes

Trug or basket

Tools

Template on page 113

Pencil

Scissors

White craft (PVA) glue

Small paintbrush

Clothespins

Ink pad and stamps (optional)

Sealing wax and stamp

1 Use the template on page 113 to trace 24 envelope shapes onto your brown paper, then cut out with scissors. Fold and glue the bottom and sides of your envelope and hold them shut using clothespins. Let dry.

2 Cut out various pictures to decorate the envelopes. Look for shapes to cut out such as a tree or heart from one type of paper and then lay that over another type of paper so that you are building up different textures and colors.

3 Add a number from 1–24 to each envelope—I added mine using an ink pad and number stamps but you could write them on.

4 Cover the whole of the front of each envelope with the matt varnish so that all edges are sealed. Let dry.

5 Place a wrapped gift in each envelope and fold the top down to close the envelope. Carefully light the sealing wax stick and let the wax drip onto the envelope—about five drips will be enough. Quickly press the sealing stamp onto the wax and hold for a few seconds. Remove the stick and your envelope is sealed!

6 Gather all the envelopes together and randomly place in your trug or basket and let the joy begin!

QUICK IDEA: GLITTER JARS

These are a really simple make that add a magical element to any mantel or table. I use a glitter that, when applied to glass, really looks like frost! However, any glitter that you put on glass will give this illusion, so even if you are not enjoying a snowy vacation, you can imagine you are by making these wintery jars.

MATERIALS

Clean glass jars
Paper
Glitter
String or florist's wire
Jingle bells
Tea lights

Tools

Scissors
Paintbrush
White craft (PVA) glue

1 If you wish to make a jar that has a design on it, first cut out a shape such as a star (either freehand or use the template on page 115) or a Christmas tree and lightly attach it with glue to the jar. (Alternatively you can just cover the whole jar with glitter, which is just as effective.)

2 Paint glue over all of the rest of the jar and immediately sprinkle on the glitter. Shake the jar to make sure that the glitter has adhered to the glass. Let it dry. When dry, carefully peel away the stencil you made to reveal your design.

3 Wrap the jar mouth with either string or wire, add some jingle bells, and tie or twist to secure. Add a tea light to bring magic to your room.

BOBBIN DECORATIONS

It is amazing what you can find sitting in your drawers at home. Often by looking at things in a different way you can create something new. I love using things that have done their job but still look charming, such as this old bobbin. The thread has been used up long ago but the shape and color of the wooden bobbin stopped me from just throwing it away. A little wire, some bells, and a tiny piece of paper is all you need to give it a chance to be useful again. As well as a tree decoration this would also make a great gift topper for a friend who loves sewing!

MATERIALS

Old wooden bobbin

Scrap of giftwrap

12 in. (30 cm) sturdy wire (or use 24 in./60 cm florist's wire, fold in half, and twist to make a thicker wire)

2 small jingle bells

Tools

Scissors

White craft (PVA) glue

1. Take your giftwrap and measure out how much you will need to cover the central part of the bobbin. Cut the giftwrap and glue it onto the bobbin.

2. Attach the bells to the wire by simply pushing the wire through the bells.

3. Thread the wire through the bobbin and make a hook at the top. Fold the bottom of the wire back up past the bells and push the end into the bobbin.

DANISH PAPER CONES

In Denmark trees are often decorated with paper cones filled with candies, greenery, or little gifts. They jolly up the tree and add an element of surprise for the family. This project shows you how to make them using what you have in your home. I think they make delightful take-home gifts after a holiday party, too. In the past, I have given guests a cone filled with tiny homemade cookies; it was a charming and delightful gift that was easy and fun to make.

MATERIALS

Thick artist paper or card stock

Selection of decorative papers, giftwrap, old sheet music

Ribbon

Tissue paper

Candies or small gifts, to fill the cone

Tools

Template on page 115

Pencil

Scissors

White craft (PVA) glue

Clothespins

1 Using the cone template on page 115, trace the shape of the cone onto the card stock and cut out the shape. Glue the sides together to form a cone and use a clothespin to hold the seam closed until it dries.

2 Cut out small pieces of pretty Christmas paper and glue them all over the cone, overlapping them in places. When the cone is completely covered, let it dry.

3. Cut a piece of ribbon to form a handle for the cone. Add a dab of glue to each end and again use clothespins to hold the ribbon in place until the glue has dried.

4. Use some tissue paper to decorate the inside of the cone and add your little candies or gifts.

STAR GARLAND

A festive garland is so useful to have when decorating your house for Christmas. I am always finding new places in my home where a little garland would just make an area more special. The key is to make a garland that is simple enough to enhance your décor rather than overpower it. They are great on banisters wrapped around some greenery as I have done here, on the Christmas tree, down the center of the table, around mirrors—wherever you feel you need a little extra decoration.

MATERIALS

Old sheet music (preferably Christmas songs!) or any other decorative paper

Florist's wire

Tools

Templates on page 115
Pencil
Scissors
White craft (PVA) glue
Clothespins

1 Using the templates on page 115, trace and draw several stars in different sizes on your paper. For every 1 yd/1 m of garland you will need about 5–7 stars. Remember that you will need two matching paper stars for each star on the wire. Cut out the stars with scissors.

2 Cut the florist's wire to your desired length. Place some glue on a star, position the wire on top, and place a matching star onto the first star, trapping the wire inside. Secure with a clothespin. Continue along the wire. Remove all the clothespins when the glue is dry. Have fun decorating

QUICK IDEA: STAMPED GIFTWRAP

Wrapped presents nestling under the Christmas tree are just so much sweeter when the giftwrap is homemade. Everyone can join in with this make. Put on those Christmas carols and stamp away!

MATERIALS

Roll of brown Kraft (parcel) paper or other plain brown giftwrap

Tools

Heavy books

Ink pad and stamps

1 Get your little ones to help you with this—it's very hard to go wrong! Unroll a length of brown paper, either along a table or on the floor. It is best to stamp on the wrong side of the paper as the right side is often shiny and the ink won't stick as well. Use heavy books to hold the paper in place.

2 Use Christmas-themed stamps to decorate your paper. Stars look good in random clusters, or you could stamp a more uniform pattern. Allow the ink to dry before using the paper to wrap your gifts.

QUICK IDEA: STAMPED CLOTHESPINS

Is it not wonderful when you can use ordinary household things to create something unique? These clothespins are stamped with little designs and are completed in the blink of an eye! They add a special touch to a present. I have also made simple fabric bags to hold several clothespins and given them as a Christmas surprise. They are also very useful in the pantry to keep opened bags of sugar or flour closed.

MATERIALS

Wooden clothespins

Tools

Ink pad and stamps

1 Simply use the ink pad and stamps to add pretty motifs to the flat side of your clothespins.

2 Allow to dry and then use the clothespins to attach cards, tags, or some Christmas greenery to your gifts.

CHAPTER TWO
NATURAL CHRISTMAS

Walking outside during the festive season is truly invigorating. You can see your breath, your cheeks get all rosy, and the houses all glow with Christmas lights. The anticipation of coming back into the warmth creates such a sense of *hygge*. Add to this picture a bag full of lovely pine cones, branches, greenery, and twigs that you have collected—you now have the elements to create Christmas the natural way. Foraging for these gifts from nature can be a joyful expedition with all the family. Pack a picnic, fill a thermos with hot chocolate, dress for the weather, and head outside.

CRAB APPLE WREATH

MATERIALS

About 1 yd/1 m florist's wire
Crab apples
Holly sprig
Lemon juice

Tools

Scissors

You may be lucky enough to have a small apple or crab apple tree in your garden; if not, try foraging for them the next time you are walking in the forest. I find the smallest ones last the longest and are very easy to thread onto the wire. Just be aware that birds love crab apples so you may decide to display this inside to stop them nibbling it!

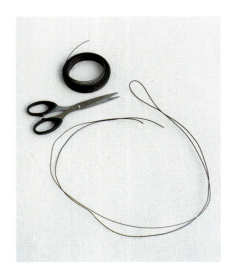

1 Decide how large you want your wire wreath to be, work out the circumference, and cut a piece of wire to double that length. Fold in half and shape into a rough circle to make sure it is the right size.

2 Start threading crab apples onto the wire: push the two cut ends into the first crab apple and thread it along the wire. Continue adding crab apples along the wire, leaving a loop of wire at one end.

3 Keep threading the apples until the ring is full, then twist the two cut ends of the wire around the looped end to secure. Shape the wreath into a circle and add some holly sprigs at the top, securing them with short pieces of wire. In order for the wreath to remain fresh for a long period of time, it is a good idea to place some drops of lemon juice on the apples where they have been pricked.

✻ Remember, I warned you about the birds so be careful where you place your wreath!

QUICK IDEA: HYACINTH BULBS IN A TIN

Hyacinths play a large part in Scandinavian Christmas celebrations. They are the flower of choice and are always dotted about the house. I think they make a lovely take-home gift after a festive party. Wrapped in old sheet music and wire, they are easy to hand out and look lovely on their own, or pop a few into a tin.

MATERIALS

Hyacinth bulbs
Old sheet music
Wire
Old baking tin

Tools

Pencil

1 Wrap each individual hyacinth bulb in paper—sheet music looks really pretty but any decorative paper will do.

2 Encircle the paper-covered bulb with wire. I like to give the wire a little twirl at the end. This is easy to do—just take a pencil and tightly wrap the end of the wire around it. Remove the pencil and put the wrapped bulbs in an old baking tin.

QUICK IDEA: HEART PILLAR CANDLES

Christmas is such a busy time of year and sometimes at the last minute you realize that you need one more present. This simple yet delightful quick idea will save the day—I do not know anyone who would not appreciate more candles at Christmas! Adding the heart and string gives the candles some homespun warmth, which is so important at this time of year.

MATERIALS

Pretty paper or old sheet music
Pillar candles
String or twine

Tools

Template on page 112
Scissors
White craft (PVA) glue

1. Cut out two little hearts (either freehand or use the template on page 112) from some pretty paper and glue them together.

2. Attach them around the candle with two loops of string and you are done.

LITTLE FOREST ADVENT CANDLE TIN

Decorating for Christmas is always a joyous task but sometimes you want something different for the table or mantelpiece. You only need to look in your cooking pans drawer, find some snippets of fabric, and go for a walk in the forest to create this next project. The tins that I have used are ones that I have picked up at the many wonderful vintage fairs that spring up throughout the year. Often, I will buy something because I simply cannot resist it and then when I get it home it suddenly dawns on me what I can use it for—such a great feeling! See what you can find to make your own unique decoration.

MATERIALS

Long shallow tin
4 tea light holders
Oasis block
Moss
Pine cones
Scraps of fabric
Whole cloves
Matchsticks
Tea lights
Glitter
Fake snow

Tools

Craft knife
Scissors
Needle and sewing thread

1 Space the tea light holders (I used vintage tins here) out in your long shallow tin and then use a craft knife to cut three pieces of oasis to fit snugly in between each one.

2 Start adding moss to the tin, arranging it around the tea light holders so it covers the oasis.

3 Add several pine cones of different sizes, pushing them into the oasis to hold in place. Some of my pine cones were sprayed white to give a different effect.

4 To make a tree, cut two small triangles from the fabric scraps. Place together and blanket stitch (see page 108) down the two long sides of the triangle. Insert a few whole cloves to give the tree some thickness and a lovely scent, and then insert the end of the matchstick into the triangle. Stitch the triangle shut. Repeat to make as many trees as you wish.

5 Dot the triangle trees here and there in the oasis. Place tea lights in the holders and then sprinkle glitter and fake snow over the top to finish your little forest.

QUICK IDEA: APPLE TEA LIGHTS

Candles are very much a part of Christmas and I can never have enough of them scattered about my home, both inside and out. They provide a welcome glow like nothing else and give you the warmest of feelings. These candle holders are simply apples carved out to fit a tea light. They are perfect on a mantelpiece or your dining table with ivy and holly, or outside on your steps or porch. They certainly create *hygge*.

MATERIALS
The reddest apples you can find
Tea lights
Lemon juice

Tools
Sharp knife
Teaspoon

1 Use a sharp knife to cut a circle out of the top of each apple, roughly the same size as a tea light.

2 Use a teaspoon to scoop out the apple—just enough so the tea light fits snugly inside. Squeeze some lemon juice around the cut edges of the apple (this will prevent them from going brown).

3 Fit the tea lights inside the apples and display on a level surface.

PINE CONE FAMILY

These little characters will add a lot of charm to your Christmas decorating. They look sweet from any angle, making them ideal to hang from a tree. Each time you make one, you will be tempted to give it a name because they really do take on a personality, particularly when made with treasured fabric scraps that you can't bear to throw away. How special would it be to receive a little forest family for Christmas?

MATERIALS

Fabric scraps in coordinating colors

Several pine cones (see Tip on page 46)

Hazelnuts

Florist's wire, jingle bells, felt pieces, to embellish

Invisible thread

Tools

Scissors

Small paintbrush

Strong white (PVA) glue

Needle and coordinating sewing thread

Muffin pans

1 Cut out strips of fabric for the clothing. The exact measurements will depend on the size of the pine cone but for a medium-sized pine cone use the following as a guide:
1 x skirt piece approx. 8 x 2½ in. (20 x 6 cm)
1 x apron piece approx. 3 x 1½ in. (8 x 4 cm)
2 x arm pieces approx. 8 x 1 in. (20 x 2.5 cm)
1 x scarf piece 3 x ½ in. (8 x 1 cm)
1 x kerchief triangle approx. 2½ in. (6 cm)

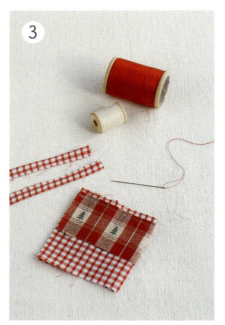

2. Glue the kerchief triangle onto a hazelnut, making sure that the face (the lighter brown area) is showing. Set aside to dry.

3. Position the apron in the center of the skirt piece so that the top edges are lined up. Using a needle and matching sewing thread, sew the apron onto the skirt with a backstitch (see page 108), then fold the skirt in half, right sides together, and sew along the side seam to form a tube. Turn out the right way. For the arms, fold the two long strips in half and backstitch along the long edges (don't worry about turning out the right way).

4. Carefully push the skirt onto the pine cone (pine cones are quite sturdy so you can be quite firm). Adjust the skirt so that you are happy with the way it looks. Sit the pine cone person in a muffin pan—this will make it easier to add any embellishments.

5. Add a generous amount of glue to the arms and stick to the pine cone. Let dry; if the arms seem too long you can easily trim them later. Tie the scarf to the neck area and add any embellishments such as a garland or a jingle bell. Finally, attach some invisible thread to the top of the kerchief to hang it.

❋ *If your pine cones are tightly shut, put them somewhere warm overnight. They will open up and be ready to be made into something wonderful.*

QUICK IDEA: SIMPLE WIRE WREATH

If you are anything like me, you love having wreaths everywhere at this time of year. This wreath is very simple to make so why not make several to hang on the backs of chairs, doors, bedposts—anywhere your imagination takes you.

MATERIALS

About 1 yd/1 m sturdy florist's wire

Greenery

Bells

Tools

Wire snips

1 Decide how large you want your wreath to be, work out the circumference, and cut a piece of wire to that length. Make a circle from your wire and twist the ends together to secure.

2 Cut several lengths of wire about 8 in. (20 cm) long. Thread a couple of jingle bells onto each piece of wire.

3 Take a piece of greenery, put it on the wire circle and use the smaller wire with bells on it to secure the greenery to the wire. Keep working all the way around until the wreath is complete.

TWIG TREE

I love the magic that glitter and sparkles create when decorating for Christmas, particularly when combined with natural items that can be found just outside your front door. These twig trees are ideal to use as a centerpiece on your dining room table. Elegant or rustic, this project will give your décor a cozy winter feel.

MATERIALS

Oasis block

Terra cotta pot

Straight twig, about 15 in. (38 cm) long

Moss

Selection of small pine cones

Selection of smaller twigs

String or twine

Florist's wire

Glitter

Stars made from found birch bark

Tools

Craft knife

Wire scissors

1 Cut a piece of the oasis block to fit snugly inside your terra cotta pot. Stick the main twig, which will act as the trunk of the tree, into the oasis.

2 Cover the oasis with moss, then arrange small pine cones over the moss.

3 Take several shorter twigs and make them into bundles by tying with string or twine. Tie each bundle onto the main "trunk" with string, making sure that each bundle is shorter the higher up they go to make a triangle shape. Tweak and adjust the twig bundles gently to get the look you want.

4 Wrap lengths of florist's wire around tiny pine cones and create a hook at the end. Hang on the twig branches to act as decorations.

5 Sprinkle some glitter on the pine cones. Add a bark star to the top of the tree. Remember, never pull bark from a living tree as this is its skin and you could kill the tree. Florists have bark stars for sale if you cannot find any bark on the forest floor.

QUICK IDEA: ANISE WREATH

This quick idea is simple and charming. Star anise can be found in the herb and spice section in any grocery store. I love the star shape of this whole spice; I intentionally decided not to cover the whole wire here—it's nice to see each delicate shape clearly.

MATERIALS

Thin florist's wire
Star anise
Ribbon

Tools

Wire snips
Hot glue gun
Scissors

1 Make a few loops of the wire and twist the ends to secure.

2 Use a hot glue gun to glue the star anise randomly on the wire—it's important not to make it look too uniform.

3 Tie a length of pretty ribbon around the wire and use to hang from a closet door, in front of a mirror, or by a window.

PINE CONE FIRELIGHTERS

MATERIALS

Assortment of small tins, old molds, muffin pans, or any shallow dishes

Wax—use the ends of old candles, new candles, or wax flakes

Pine cones

Whole cloves

Glitter

24 x 9 in. (60 x 23 cm) piece of burlap (hessian) fabric

String or twine

Tools

Double boiler (or use an old saucepan set over a pan of simmering water)

White craft (PVA) glue

Needle and sewing thread (or use a sewing machine)

Roaring fires are surely part of a cozy Christmas; they are what *hygge* is all about. In order to create the perfect fire you need dry logs, paper, kindling, and natural firelighters. Having enjoyed fires wherever I have lived, I have had plenty of experience trying out what does and does not work to get that warm blaze going. These firelighters are easy to make, cost nothing, and make the most wonderful present. I make a simple burlap bag to put them in and then tie it up with string and glittered pine cones when I give them away.

The main ingredient is old wax. I collect all my ends of candles and place them in a double boiler. Heat the wax slowly and not too hot so they are just melted. Then simply follow the steps below and you will be amazed.

1 First, gather together your molds and tins. Melt your wax slowly over a low heat and then pour a small amount into one of your tins.

2 Immediately place a pine cone on top. Sprinkle some whole cloves around the pine cone. These will give off a wonderful scent when thrown into the fire.

3 Place the tins into the freezer for about an hour until the wax is completely solid. Remove from the freezer; the firelighters will then pop out of the molds leaving no residue behind. Sprinkle with some glitter for a festive feel, dabbing a little glue onto the pine cone to make it stick. They almost look good enough to eat!

4 To turn these into a lovely gift, make a simple bag for them. Fold the piece of burlap (hessian) in half, short end to short end, and simply stitch along each side seam, leaving a ½ in. (1 cm) seam allowance. Turn inside out and fill the bag. Tie a piece of string around a glittered pine cone and use it to close the bag.

5 Now all you have to do is go and build your fire. Simply scrunch up some paper, add a little kindling, and put your pine cone on top. Light the paper, watch as the pine cone catches light, and enjoy the warmth. When the kindling is burning add on your dry logs, sit back, and feel pleased with yourself!

PINE CONE FIRELIGHTERS

QUICK IDEA: IVY GARLAND

I love walking into a house and seeing a staircase covered in ivy—it is very inviting and special. Whenever I have shown this method to friends I always get the same reaction: they cannot believe how quick and easy it is to make. The garland will last for about two weeks and is as quick to remove as it is to put up.

MATERIALS

Sturdy wire
Long pieces of ivy
Other greenery, such as fir
Jingle bells (optional)

1 Wrap the wire along your banister or around a stair post.

2 Simply loosely wrap the ivy around the wire and keep adding until you have covered the wire and have created the look you want. Tuck extra pieces of greenery in amongst the ivy. I prefer a simple garland but you could add jingle bells: simply attach to lengths of wire and twist onto the garland.

QUICK IDEA: TWIG CANDLE HOLDERS

These twig candle holders add such a feeling of magic to your home you will want to make several. Any twigs will do, but those that have a little bit of lichen attached to them will catch the candlelight as it filters through. The feeling of being transported to an enchanted forest is really overwhelming and these create the perfect light to read those special Christmas stories. Collect as many twigs as you can because these candleholders look best in groups of three or more.

MATERIALS

Clean, clear glass jars in various sizes
Selection of twigs

Tools
Hot glue gun

1. Start attaching twigs to one of your jars—simply add a few dots of glue along the twig and press onto the glass.

2. Work around the jar, varying the height of the twigs to create a more natural feel.

3. Take care with the glue gun as the glue will be very hot and dries quickly.

CHAPTER THREE
HOMESPUN FABRICS

Walking into a store offering vintage or new fabrics always makes me catch my breath. It can be a tiny bundle of snippets or a simple roll of burlap but each conjures up a vision of how it can be spun into a delightful Christmas gift or decorative item. I am quite traditional: I decorate my home in red and green for Christmas, so during the year I am always on the look out for these colors when looking through antiques fairs and flea markets. Old shirts, pajamas, or tablecloths are a great source of fabric—how lovely is it to make a gift from something that belonged to someone else in the family. My mother once made everyone a pillow using my late father's old shirts. She made sure that each had a pocket from the shirt in the pillow. Inside was a little note dedicated to the recipient.

HEART WREATH

Hearts are a symbol of love and joy and what better time to have a heart wreath than at Christmas? This wreath may look complicated but I can assure you, it is not at all! The trick is to find a ready-made heart-shaped wreath—try craft or home decorating stores, or florists. If you like hunting around flea markets and antique fairs, you will find vintage wooden bobbins that need a new home. Craft stores are also a good source for new wooden bobbins for making and creating.

MATERIALS

Selection of wooden bobbins in assorted sizes

Ribbons and trims in assorted widths

Scraps of decorative paper or giftwrap

Heart-shaped wreath

Tools

Scissors

Fabric glue

Hot glue gun

White craft (PVA) glue

1 Using the ribbons, trims, and papers, decorate all of the bobbins: wrap ribbon around the bobbins and secure with fabric glue or the hot glue gun. For an alternative look, use white craft (PVA) glue to stick scraps of decorative paper to the bobbins. Allow to dry.

2 Lay your wreath on a flat surface. Use a hot glue gun to dab some glue onto the wreath and immediately press on a bobbin. Arrange the bobbins at different angles to create interest but also make sure that you can see the decorated part of the bobbin. Take care as the glue will be very hot.

4

3 Continue adding bobbins until you are happy with your wreath.

4 Choose a complementary ribbon and tie onto the top of the wreath for hanging. You can also tie a larger, decorative ribbon to the bottom of the heart.

5 Check each bobbin making sure it is secure and no threads are left hanging. Now all that is left to do is find a place to hang it!

HOMESPUN FABRICS

QUICK IDEA: FABRIC-COVERED CANS

MATERIALS

Cans in assorted sizes
Selection of fabrics
Ribbons
Buttons
Jingle bells

Tools

Tape measure
Scissors
White craft (PVA) glue

I never seem to have enough pitchers (jugs) to put out all the greenery that I so love to have in the house at Christmas. A very quick and easy remedy is to cover some old cans with festive fabric. Choosing different sizes looks adorable when they are all grouped together. I also use mine to store bundles of candles so that they are always within reach when I need them. These make a lovely way to present flowers to your host as a gift.

1 Measure the height and circumference of the can and cut a piece of fabric to these measurements, adding ½ in. (1 cm) to the circumference.

2 Apply glue to the can and wrap the fabric around. Make sure you glue the fabric where it overlaps and press down to stick together.

3 Add ribbons, buttons, or bells to the cans to decorate.

PATCHWORK QUILT BAUBLES

Once you start this project you are never going to want to stop. It is fun to do with a group of people and a great way to use up your old fabric scraps. A lovely friend taught me how to make these in Canada many years ago. They are very light and therefore ideal to use in a garland on a staircase and safe for little hands to touch. I have chosen red as the main color, using different sizes of gingham and small prints. I have loved gingham for as long as I can remember. When my son was about five years old he told me that he knew what my favorite color was… I looked at him and waited for the answer… he smiled and said "gingham!"

MATERIALS

Selection of fabric scraps

Styrofoam balls, 2 in. (5 cm) in diameter

Baker's twine

Tools

Scissors

Sharp knife

Pins

1 Cut up several pieces of fabric. The scraps of fabric can be any size but I do think that they look best if you stick to a main color. You'll need about 4–5 pieces per bauble.

2 Take a piece of fabric and place it on the bauble. Hold the ball firmly against your work surface and, using the back of a knife, gently press the fabric edges into the ball. You do not need to go in very deep—the Styrofoam will "catch" the fabric. Repeat, adding more patches, until the entire bauble is covered.

3 Cut a piece of baker's twine about 6 in. (15 cm) long and knot together to make a hanger for the bauble. Push it into the bauble with a pin—your bauble is now ready to hang!

OLD WINDOW FRAME DISPLAY

Using something old and apparently redundant to create something new and beautiful is not only fulfilling but also great for the environment. I started collecting old window frames quite a while ago, thinking that one day I would do something with them. One day I did! These frames are great to use at Christmas to display beautiful cards, pieces of children's artwork, or to leave a message. It is easy to change the display so you can place new things in the frame to admire. I keep mine up all year and simply change the fabrics that line the window to match the season!

MATERIALS

Old window frame (check out local architectural salvage yards to find nice ones with the glass still intact)

Enough coordinating fabric to cover the windows

4 picture tacks or nails

About 20 in. (50 cm) sturdy wire (or use 1 yd/1 m florist's wire, fold in half, and twist to make a thicker wire)

Mini clothespins

Tools

Sandpaper

Tape measure

Scissors

White craft (PVA) glue

Hammer

Wire snips

Pencil

1 Place the old window on a stable flat surface and use the sandpaper to clean away and smooth all the rough edges.

2 Measure the windows and cut the fabric to fit perfectly inside each windowpane. Spread a thin layer of glue over the glass and carefully place the cut fabric on the glued windowpane.

3 Decide where you want to position the wire for hanging and hammer in the nails or tacks (I used 4 here to create hanging wires on each side of the window frame).

4 Cut the wire about 2 in. (5 cm) longer than you need it and wind around the nails. Twist the leftover wire tightly around a pencil to create the curled look to the wire. Use mini clothespins to attach cards or artworks to the wires.

QUICK IDEA: COVERED MATCHBOX

These are not only useful but also make a wonderful thoughtful present at this time of year. Covered in Christmas fabric and ribbon, they look lovely on any surface. I have made these for many years for friends and family and they are always pleased to receive them.

MATERIALS
Matchboxes in assorted sizes
Fabric
Ribbon

Tools
Scissors
White craft (PVA) glue

1 Measure around the matchbox from one side of the striking edge to the other. Cut a piece of pretty fabric to this measurement by the width of the box.

2 Glue the fabric to the matchbox outer cover, making sure the edges are lined up on either side of the striking surface. Add some pretty ribbon to finish.

FABRIC GARLAND

Christmas garlands feature in most homes during the festive season. They add a touch of seasonal color and instantly create a sense of joy when you see them. These fabric garlands can be hung anywhere, from staircases to over doorframes, on mantelpieces and around dressers. Their welcome jingle will always make people smile and the fact that they are made from fabric means they won't dry up and look sad after a few days. These are easy to make but do take some time in preparation depending how long you want your garland to be. The best thing is that, once it is made, it can be used and enjoyed year after year.

MATERIALS

String or twine

Assorted fabric pieces in coordinating colors and patterns

Silver jingle bells

Tools

Scissors

1 Decide how long you want your garland to be and cut three pieces of string or twine all to this same length. Join the three strings together by tying a knot at one end.

2 Cut several long thin pieces of fabric, each about 6 x 1 in. (15 x 2.5 cm), ready to be tied onto the strings. Tie each "ribbon" onto the strings one at a time and keep going until you have filled up the string. Knot the ends of the string.

3 Trim any knotted pieces of fabric if you like—you can make them all a uniform length or have some longer than others. Tie the bells onto some lengths of string and secure them to the garland at evenly spaced intervals.

MISTLETOE WREATH

Nothing quite welcomes people into your home like a wreath. I tend to use wreaths throughout the year but at Christmas I cannot seem to get enough of them. Real greenery is beautiful but in our warm houses they do not tend to last very long. I love the look of mistletoe but again, it dries out so quickly when indoors, so here is my everlasting mistletoe wreath. This size is just perfect to be used hanging behind a chair or in a little window. The glistening berries add just a little touch of magic to the whole look.

MATERIALS

Felt in assorted shades of green
Green gingham fabric
Scraps of gray felt
Wicker wreath, approximately 8 in. (20 cm) in diameter
Small white buttons
Glitter

Tools

Templates on page 118
Scissors
Fabric glue
Paintbrush
Hot glue gun

1 Using the mistletoe leaf templates on page 118, cut out several leaves from each of the green felts. Cut a handful of leaves from gray felt, too.

2 Use fabric glue to glue some green gingham fabric onto a piece of green felt. Cut these into more leaves.

3 Using the hot glue gun, attach the leaves to the wreath, mixing up the different colors. Make sure that the leaves are all pointing in the same direction—clockwise or counterclockwise—around the wreath.

4 Use the hot glue gun to attach small buttons for berries all around the wreath. Dab the tops of the buttons with white craft (PVA) glue and sprinkle with glitter.

CLOVE-SCENTED CHRISTMAS TREES

Once you start making these little scented Christmas trees you will be tempted to create a whole forest. Using an old screw gives them a special character and also provides some weight, which helps the tree to hang very nicely.

MATERIALS

Selection of Christmas fabric scraps

Selection of old screws

Cloves

Small silver jingle bells

String or twine

Tools

Scissors

Sewing machine

Needle and matching sewing thread

1 Cut out pairs of triangles in various sizes from the fabrics. The fabric doesn't have to be the same—it is actually very pretty to use two different fabrics for one tree—cut 2 different triangles in half and sew different pairs together to make a pieced triangle shape.

2 Put the triangles right sides together and use a sewing machine to sew the triangles together, leaving a gap at the bottom for the cloves and the screw.

3 Turn the tree inside out and pop three or four cloves inside, then insert the screw. Fold the raw edges under and slip stitch (see page 108) the opening shut.

4 Stitch a silver jingle bell to the top of the tree and then tie on a loop of string or twine for hanging.

❋ *These little trees look particularly sweet hanging from the mitten garland (see page 78). Mix them with small stockings and the garland will soon look very Christmassy!*

FRAMED CHRISTMAS PICTURES

These sweet little frames look delightful propped up against a window or on a little shelf. They add a touch of whimsy and can be adapted to suit any occasion. Add a little hook and string and you can hang them on your Christmas tree. They are light enough to be sent far and wide and are packed full of that "homemade with love" feeling.

MATERIALS

4 pieces of strip wood, each approximately 3 in. (8 cm) long

White eggshell paint

Selection of fabric snippets

Piece of linen fabric, approximately 4 in. (10 cm) square

Stranded embroidery floss (thread)

Cardboard

Piece of red gingham fabric, approximately 4 in. (10 cm) square

Tools

Paintbrushes

Hot glue gun

Needle

White craft (PVA) glue

Staple gun

1 First, paint all the pieces of wood with white eggshell paint and let dry. Add a second coat if needed. When all the pieces are dry, use a hot glue gun to attach the 4 pieces together to make a square frame. Let dry.

2 Trim the piece of linen fabric so it fits inside the frame. Now cut out a few shapes from your fabric snippets, such as a heart, a Christmas stocking, or a little house. Position the fabric picture on the linen square and blanket stitch around the edges to hold in place (see page 108).

3 Cut a piece of cardboard to fit the frame and then use white craft (PVA) glue to stick the linen to the cardboard.

4 Use a staple gun to fix the linen-covered cardboard to the back of the frame. Finally, cut the red gingham fabric to size and glue to the back of the cardboard to create a neat finish.

FRAMED CHRISTMAS PICTURES

TEA LIGHT APRON

I love aprons. I wear them all the time, but to me they are a fashion accessory, so they should be pretty as well as useful. Here at home I am always lighting tea lights, inside and out, day and night. I love to hang lanterns up outside and have been known to light several and then go across the road to look at the house… it just makes me happy. And so I had the idea for this tea light apron—one pocket for fresh tea lights, one pocket for old ones, and one pocket for matches, leaving my hands free to create my winter wonderland.

MATERIALS

Linen fabric

Red gingham fabric

Vintage dish (tea) towel, preferably red and white

Ribbon

Tools

Scissors

Pins

Sewing machine

Needle and matching sewing thread

1 Cut 2 pieces of linen fabric, each 7 x 6½ in. (18 x 16 cm). Cut a strip of red gingham fabric that is 2 x 6½ in. (5 x 16 cm).

2 Pin the red gingham strip to the short edge of one of the linen pieces and machine stitch with a ½ in. (1 cm) seam allowance. Add the second linen piece to the other edge of the gingham strip so that the gingham is stitched in the middle of the two linen pieces.

3 Now cut a piece of gingham fabric that is the same size as this stitched piece. Place the two pieces right sides together and stitch all the way around with a ½ in. (1 cm) seam allowance, leaving a gap in one short edge for turning through. Turn right side out and slip stitch (see page 108) the gap closed.

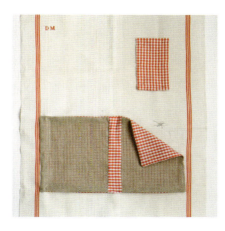

4 Pin the pocket onto the dish (tea) towel and then stitch around three sides, leaving the top open. Sew down the middle of the red gingham strip to create two pockets.

5 Repeat to make a single, smaller pocket and position above the large pocket—use red gingham fabric or any other fabric you choose.

6 Cut two lengths of ribbon to make ties for the apron, making sure that they are long enough to tie comfortably around your waist. Stitch each ribbon to the wrong side of each top corner of the apron.

❋ Why not make just one large mitten? Fill it with something special and give it as a Christmas present—simply add a little loop of ribbon so that it can be hung on a tree or doorknob as a decoration.

MITTEN GARLAND

There is something very special about these little mittens. What appeals to me is that they can be displayed as soon as the weather begins to feel wintery and then as the season progresses you can add little decorations to welcome in Christmas. Fill them with greenery, chocolate, or tiny presents. They will always delight.

MATERIALS

Felted cream woolen blanket

Red stranded embroidery floss (thread)

Ribbons, buttons, and jingle bells

Baker's twine

Mini clothespins

Tools

Templates on pages 116–117

Pins

Scissors

Needle and sewing thread

1 Using the templates on pages 116 and 117, cut out two pieces of felted woolen blanket for every mitten that you want to make. If your blanket already has an edge finished with blanket stitch, try and use it by placing the edge of your template along the edge of the blanket.

2 Stitch two matching mitten pieces together using embroidery floss (thread) and blanket stitch (see page 108), leaving the mitten open at the top.

3 Decorate your mittens by sewing on ribbons, buttons, and bells—add as much or as little decoration as you like.

4 Attach the mittens to a length of baker's twine using mini clothespins.

MITTEN GARLAND 79

HYGGE WOOL BAG

Trying to think of a thoughtful present for friends or family can sometimes be difficult, so here is a simple idea that is easy to make and will certainly give lots of joy throughout the season and beyond. It is easy to adapt depending on the recipient—spices, soaps, or whatever you think they will enjoy will work. Just pop them into the bag and send it on with love.

MATERIALS

Old woolen blanket

Red embroidery floss (thread)

Gingham fabric

New pair of wool socks (for the recipient)

Long candles

Tea lights

Small sock for decoration

Silver jingle bells

Small covered matchbox (see page 67)

Tools

Scissors

Sewing machine

Needle and sewing thread

Baker's twine

1 Cut 2 squares of fabric from the woolen blanket, each one approximately 12 in. (30 cm) square. Cut 2 pieces of gingham fabric, each one approximately 8 in. (20 cm) square.

2 Place the two blanket square right sides together and, with a ½ in. (1 cm) seam allowance, machine stitch around three sides of the square. (My blanket was already finished with blanket stitch but you can add your own along the top edge with red embroidery floss (thread), see page 108.)

3 Repeat with the gingham squares to make a gingham bag. Turn over a small double hem to the wrong side and machine stitch around the top of the bag. Turn both bags the right way out.

❄ *Who wouldn't appreciate a homemade bag full of everything you need to create a relaxing ambience?*

4 Put the long candles inside the wool socks and fill the gingham bag with the tea lights. Tie the gingham bag shut with a length of baker's twine and add a bell.

5 Sew the small sock for decoration and a small bell onto the wool bag.

6 Place the filled socks and gingham bag inside the wool bag and tie the wool bag shut with baker's twine and bell. Finish by putting a pretty covered matchbox into the small sock.

EMBROIDERED HAND TOWELS

During the year I am always on the look out for things that can be made into Christmas presents and I can never pass up a chance to buy old but beautiful European hand towels. They have a wonderful soft feel and they often come in red and cream colors, making them perfect to use at this time of year. Make sure that they are stain free.

MATERIALS

Clean hand or dish (tea) towels
Red stranded embroidery floss (thread)
Narrow ribbon
Small buttons
Small silver jingle bells

Tools
Templates on page 119
Washable fabric pen
Needle

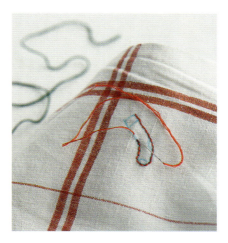

1. Using a washable fabric pen, draw some simple Christmas motifs onto the corner of each towel, or use the templates on page 119.

2. Using stranded embroidery floss (thread) and a simple backstitch (see page 108), embroider your design onto the towel.

3. Cut a short length of ribbon, fold it in half, and stitch to the corner of the towel. I add a button to the back of the loop and a bell to the front for strength, as it will receive a lot of use.

CHRISTMAS STOCKINGS

A Christmas stocking is a special tradition that seems to have been embraced by everyone. To keep with the Scandinavian feel, I have made this one from an old red and white quilt that was really too ruined to be used or displayed. I love reusing things that seem ready to be thrown out. With just a little imagination the quilt was reinvented into something lovely.

MATERIALS

Old red and white quilt

Pattern paper for template

Red and silver stranded embroidery floss (thread)

Ribbons and decorative trimmings

Silver jingle bells

Tools

Templates on pages 119 and 120

Pins

Scissors

Washable fabric pen

Sewing machine

Needle

1 Transfer the template on page 120 onto your pattern paper and use it to cut out two stocking shapes from the quilt, remembering to flip the pattern so you have two pieces that will fit right sides together. Use pins to hold the template in place.

2 Draw some simple Christmas designs onto the quilt using a fabric pen, or use the templates on pages 119 and 120, and then embroider them using a simple satin stitch (see page 111).

3 Refer to the stitch guide on page 120 to add further embroidery details using backstitch, detached chain stitch, and French knots (see pages 108 and 111). I like to mix in some metallic thread here and there to give a little sparkle when the stocking catches the light. It is very subtle but very sweet.

4 Sew the two stocking pieces right sides together, taking a ½ in. (1 cm) seam allowance and leaving the top open. Fold a small hem to the wrong side to cover any raw edges on the top edge and stitch. Turn right side out.

5 Fold a short length of ribbon in half to make a loop and then stitch to the top of the stocking. Add lengths of ribbon or other decorative trims as desired and finish with a few jingle bells.

QUICK IDEA: JAR COVERS

Jelly or jam jar covers have been done before in various forms but I have added a tiny button to the middle of the fabric cover so that you can attach a little tag to the jar. I find that this is much easier than tying the tag directly onto the jar and it is nicer to read. These will look charming on any Christmas morning table, whether you're using homemade or store-bought preserves. I love using baker's twine and it's perfect for tying these covers onto jars.

MATERIALS

Selection of Christmas fabrics
Buttons
Small paper luggage tags
Baker's twine

Tools

Pinking shears
Needle and sewing thread

1. Use pinking shears to cut out squares of coordinating fabrics, each approximately 8 x 8 in. (20 x 20 cm).

2. Sew a button onto the middle of the fabric.

3. Write out your tags and attach to the button using lengths of baker's twine. Secure the fabric to a jar with a length of baker's twine, tied in a bow.

CHRISTMAS TREE PILLOW

A very easy way to redecorate your home every season is to change your pillows (cushions). It is one of my favorite things that we make at The Cozy Club. I tend to have a few Christmas workshops and one is usually creating a Christmas pillow. It is lovely to receive as a gift but is also a pretty way to get your home into the Christmas spirit.

MATERIALS

4 different coordinating fabrics

11 in. (28 cm) square of linen fabric for the center of the pillow

17 in. (42 cm) square of backing fabric

Scrap of green gingham fabric

Fusible bonding web

Green, red, white, and silver embroidery floss (thread)

Selection of buttons

Silver jingle bell

16 in. (40 cm) square feather pillow insert

Tools

Template on page 121

Scissors

Pins

Sewing machine and matching sewing thread

Pencil

Iron

Needle

1 Cut out and assemble your pieces of fabric for the front of the pillow—you will need to cut four strips of fabric measuring 17 x 5 in. (42 x 12 cm) that will be stitched to the center panel to make a wide border, including 1 in. (2.5 cm) for seam allowances.

2 Start by pinning the first strip to the center linen panel right sides together. Position the strip so that it overlaps the square by ½ in. (1 cm) at one edge and by 5½ in. (12.5 cm) at the other side. Using a sewing machine, stitch the pieces together, leaving a ½ in. (1 cm) seam allowance. Repeat to add the next strip. You should end up with a square approximately 17 x 17 in. (42 x 42 cm).

HOMESPUN FABRICS

3 Following the manufacturer's instructions, fuse the fusible bonding web to the wrong side of the green gingham fabric. Copy the template on page 121. Fold the fabric in half, place the template on the fold, and use a pencil to draw around the tree shape; cut out the tree.

4 Peel the backing away from the back of the tree and lay onto the right side of the linen square so that it is positioned in the center of the pillow. Following the instructions, use a hot iron to fuse the fabrics together.

5 Using blanket stitch (see page 108) and green embroidery floss (thread), sew around the tree. Using red embroidery floss and running stitch (see page 108), sew around the outside of the tree.

6 Using silver embroidery floss, add several buttons to the tree. Add a silver bell to the top of the tree. Finally, create the illusion of snowflakes by stitching French knots (see page 111) over the surface of the linen fabric.

7 Place the front piece and backing piece right sides together and pin together. Sew all around the edges with a ½ in. (1 cm) seam allowance, leaving a gap in one edge to insert the pillow form. Trim the seam allowance and press the seams open, then turn the cover right way out.

8 Insert the pillow form and then slip stitch (see page 108) the opening closed.

You can use the same technique to create many different pillows of different sizes. A few pillows with coordinating fabrics create a lovely scene for Christmas.

TOMTE or LITTLE NISSE

It is very common to see these little characters dotted around homes in Scandinavia. They never fail to make you smile. You can just imagine them hiding in the woods...

MATERIALS

Wooden bobbins
Red acrylic paint
Felt in assorted colors (red, gray, black)
Stranded embroidery floss (thread)
Small silver bells
White wool roving
Small buttons

Tools

Template on page 121
Paintbrush
Scissors
Needle
Hot glue gun

1 Paint the wooden bobbins using red acrylic paint and leave to dry completely.

2 Copy the template on page 121. Fold a piece of felt in half and pin the hat template on the fold. Cut around the template (do not cut the folded part).

3 Fold the hat in half and stitch along the long edge (leave the bottom open) using blanket stitch (see page 108). When you get to the top of the hat, add a small silver bell. You can also blanket stitch around the rim, if you like.

4 Using the hot glue gun, attach the wool roving to the bobbin along with the button (this will be the nose of the Tomte). Place some glue along the inner edge of the felt hat and press the hat firmly onto the bobbin. Make sure that the little nose is just peeping out from under his hat.

It is quite amazing how these little ones put everyone in a good mood. They are small enough to be concealed in obscure places and when discovered, a little chuckle can be heard from the person who found them.

QUICK IDEA: LITTLE EMBROIDERED DECORATIONS

These sweet little decorations are made quite quickly using leftover fabric pieces. The embroidery does not have to be intricate and can be done freehand. A simple motif on white fabric makes them clearly visible on the Christmas tree. Whenever I give a present I like to hang something on top along with the card. It just adds a "wrapped with love" feel to the gift.

MATERIALS

Linen fabric scraps

Stranded embroidery floss (thread)

Stuffing (I use scraps of leftover fabric—a great way to avoid waste!)

Tools

Scissors

Needle and matching sewing thread

1 Cut two rectangles of linen approximately 3 x 2 in. (8 x 5 cm).

2 Using stranded embroidery floss (thread), embroider a little Christmas motif onto one of the pieces of linen. Use backstitch and French knots (see pages 108 and 111) and don't worry if the design looks homemade—that's part of the charm!

3 Sew a little knot into each corner of the fabric and leave the ends visible to give it a special look.

4 Place the two pieces of linen right sides together and backstitch (see page 108) around the edges, leaving a gap for turning. Turn the right way out and push some stuffing or fabric scraps through the gap. Slip stitch (see page 108) closed and then add a loop of thread for hanging.

EMBROIDERED CHRISTMAS NAPKINS

There will always be a time when you need just one more present and this idea will come in very handy. Stock up on Christmas fabric napkins at the end of the season and you can relax knowing that you can make something with love in no time at all!

MATERIALS

Small piece of linen
Fusible bonding web
Stranded embroidery floss (thread)
4 ready-made napkins
4 small silver jingle bells

Tools

Templates on page 119
Scissors
Iron
Washable fabric pen
Sewing machine
Needle and matching sewing thread

1 Following the manufacturer's instructions, fuse the fusible bonding web to the linen fabric. Cut 4 small squares from this fabric, each one approximately 1¼ x 1¼ in. (3 x 3 cm).

2 Using the templates on page 119, draw a small Christmas motif onto each square and then embroider the motif onto the square using stranded embroidery floss (thread). Use a combination of backstitch and satin stitch (see pages 108 and 111).

❋ *A bundle of napkins will be a very welcome and useful present for the Christmas season. You can use the same technique to make monogrammed napkins for an even more personalized gift.*

3 Peel the bonding web backing away from the fabric and iron each square onto the corner of a napkin.

4 Using a sewing machine and a small zigzag stitch, stitch around the square to hold in place on the napkin.

5 Add a small silver bell to each little square and you're done!

QUICK IDEA: MINI STOCKINGS

MATERIALS

Old quilt pieces
Stranded embroidery floss (thread)
Tiny silver jingle bell

Tools

Template on page 121
Scissors
Needle

I cannot throw away any fabric—even tiny little pieces. I always think that one day I will find a use for them. I often buy old quilts that have seen better days and when I look at them all worn and tattered, I think they must have kept someone warm and cozy for many years. Knowing that a quilt cannot be displayed anymore, I try to think of ways to reuse it. These make perfect present toppers as well as lovely decorations for the tree.

1 Using the template on page 121, cut a mini stocking shape from your old quilt fabric.

2 Using stranded embroidery floss (thread) in a contrasting color, work a running stitch (see page 108) around the edge of the shape.

3 Add a little silver bell to the top and a loop for hanging.

CHAPTER FOUR
CINNAMON AND GINGERBREAD

Gingerbread ignites the passion for Christmas baking in me. Whether for eating or decoration, cinnamon, ginger, and cloves evoke the scent of a rural Scandinavian farmhouse. Childhood memories return and one can picture the mixing, rolling, and cookie cutting. The excitement of that special season is fast approaching. I vividly remember baking with Nicholas and Stefan, my two young sons. We all treasure these family memories. In this chapter the projects will help you to make enchanting decorations with your family and friends. Icing and edible glitter will add the finishing touches to your own kitchen table creations.

GINGERBREAD HANGING DECORATIONS

I have been making these gingerbread decorations for years to liven up my little tree in the kitchen. I also use them to decorate gifts and often put several into old mason jars to be given as gifts themselves. Salt dough is a lovely way to make cinnamon-scented decorations that will last and last—even if you can't eat them! As with the star wreath on page 106, they need to be stored in an airtight container. The lovely warm Christmassy scent will be released every time you open the jar.

MATERIALS

Ingredients

1 cup (8 oz/225 g) all-purpose (plain) flour

¾ cup (6 oz/180 g) mix of ground cinnamon and cloves, plus extra for dusting

Scant 1 cup (8 oz/225 g) table salt

1 cup (8 fl oz/240 ml) water

Tools

Cookie cutters

Baking sheet

Scissors

Baker's twine

1. Preheat the oven to 225°F (110°C/gas mark ¼). Put all the ingredients into a bowl and mix until the dough is smooth and not sticky. If it does feel sticky, add more ground spices not flour. The dough is ready to use when the rough feel of salt has gone.

2. Lightly dust a board or surface with ground spices (not flour) and roll out the dough. Using spices will give the dough a "gingerbread" look.

3. Use cookie cutters to cut out shapes and lay them on the baking sheet (no need to grease). Remember to poke a hole in the top of the decorations BEFORE you bake them. Bake in the oven for about 3–4 hours until they harden; don't be tempted to bake on a higher heat or they will crack and break. Remove from the oven and let cool.

4. Cut a piece of twine (I like to use red and white baker's twine), fold it in half and thread the loop through the hole in the top of the decoration. Thread the two tails through the loop and pull up to secure. Your decorations are now ready to hang!

GINGERBREAD HANGING DECORATIONS

GINGERBREAD HOUSE

Who doesn't love walking into a room and seeing a little house all decorated in what looks like snow glittering in the candlelight? Whether we are young or old, a gingerbread house always gets our full, undivided attention and everyone is filled with delight. However, the prospect of making one often brings to mind cracking gingerbread, collapsing walls, or dripping wet frosting everywhere. I am here to tell you that this gingerbread house is fun, easy, and always works. This is the recipe that I have used for many years. Most gingerbread recipes call for molasses but I use corn (golden) syrup... what a revelation! It makes the dough so much easier to work with and it bakes flat. I also add a lot more spices... it is Christmas after all!

For the gingerbread

1 cup (7 oz/215 g) packed soft dark brown sugar

½ cup (6 fl oz/180 ml) corn (golden) syrup

1 stick (4 oz/115 g) unsalted butter

2 tbsp ground cinnamon

2 tbsp ground ginger

½ tsp salt

1¼ cups (½ pint/300 ml) milk

7¾ cups (2¼ lb/975 g) all-purpose (plain) flour

1 tbsp baking powder

Templates on pages 122–123

For the royal icing

6 egg whites

7 cups (2 lb/900 g) confectioner's (icing) sugar

1 tsp cream of tartar

1. Put the sugar, syrup, butter, spices, and salt into a pan, place over a low heat and melt together. Add the milk and stir well. Let cool. Put the flour and baking powder into a large bowl, add the wet ingredients, and mix well. (You can do this by hand or using a mixer; just work until the dough pulls away from the mixing bowl easily.) Divide the dough in half, wrap each half in plastic wrap (cling film) and place in the refrigerator overnight. (The dough will keep like this for several days.)

2. When you are ready to bake, remove the dough from the refrigerator while you preheat the oven to 325°F (160°C/gas mark 3) and lightly grease a baking sheet. Put a piece of baking parchment on top of the baking sheet and grease that too (this makes it easier to roll the dough). When the dough has been out of the refrigerator for about 15 minutes start rolling. Roll out the dough to about ¾ in. (2 cm) and then use the templates on pages 122–123 to cut out all shapes that you want baked. Remove the offcuts from the baking parchment (you can use these for something else) and bake the cut pieces in the oven for 10 minutes. Let the baked pieces cool completely, ideally overnight (they should be hard when you start building).

3. While the gingerbread is cooling make the royal icing—by far the best way to glue your house together. Put the egg whites into a very clean mixing bowl, making sure there is no grease at all in the bowl. Use a hand-held electric whisk to beat the egg whites until soft peaks form, then add the sugar and cream of tartar and keep whisking for about 10 minutes until the icing is stiff. This icing is amazing. I have made it and kept it in my pantry for a few days covered with a damp clean cloth to prevent it from drying out. When I want to use it I simply give it a quick mix and it is ready to be used again.

MATERIALS

Wooden board
White parchment paper
Baked gingerbread pieces
Edible tiny silver balls
Marshmallow pieces
Cinnamon sticks
Edible glitter

Tools

Frosting syringe or piping bag and fine tip (nozzle)
Round-bladed knife
Two tall glass tumblers

1 Find a suitable flat board like a wooden cutting board and cover it with white baking parchment. This gives you a solid surface on which to build the house and also resembles snow when you start to decorate.

2 I find that if you decorate the pieces before you actually construct the house it is easier and more fun to do. Transfer some royal icing to a frosting syringe or piping bag fitted with a fine tip (nozzle) and start piping around the edges. Add lines, dots, scallops—whatever you like.

3 Use a round-bladed knife to spread a thick layer of royal icing over the two roof pieces. Add embellishment to the roof with dots or swirls.

4 Now have some fun by adding silver bells or edible glitter to your iced pieces. You could even attach some smaller pieces of gingerbread. Leave all your iced pieces to dry for a couple of hours or even overnight.

5 Put lots of icing along the bases of the triangles and position them on the parchment-covered board. Use two tumblers to hold them in position.

6 Add the roof pieces using lots of icing. There may be a gap where the roof pieces meet at the top but you can easily cover any cracks with extra gingerbread pieces or icing. Allow to dry.

7 Now you can have fun and use your imagination on what your house needs for decoration. I like to add gingerbread trees, pieces of marshmallow, silver balls, and cinnamon sticks. I have added an old metal Father Christmas for a little touch of color. My favorite part comes when I dust it with edible glitter. I light some candles around the little house and the sparkle makes you feel like you have walked into an enchanted forest.

GINGERBREAD SALT DOUGH WREATH

This has to be one of my favorite things to make at Christmas time. The sweet cinnamon scent transports me into a magical Christmas world. The salt dough itself can be made into many different things from wreaths, tree decorations, garlands, and present toppers and if stored properly, these decorations release their aroma from year to year. I have given these to many of my friends and family and they are always received with joy. Use the recipe on page 100 and follow the instructions for rolling and baking in the oven.

MATERIALS

36 gingerbread salt dough stars (see page 100)
Star cookie cutter
Hot glue gun
Confectioner's (icing) sugar and/or glitter, for dusting
String
Silver jingle bells

Tools

Small strainer or sieve
Small spoon

1. Place all of your stars in a pile and start laying out a circle. Using the hot glue gun, add a drop of glue on the tip of a star, and place another star tip on top of it. Continue until you have the circle size you want. Please make sure that you let the glue dry before attempting to move the wreath. The glue is also very hot, so do this step carefully.

2. Keep adding stars to add two more layers to the circle shape. Let the wreath dry for a minute—it dries very quickly!

3 Dust the stars with some confectioner's (icing) sugar and/or glitter. I find using an old tea strainer and teaspoon gives the look of a light dusting of snow to the wreath.

4 Tie some silver jingle bells onto a few lengths of string and then loosely tie around the wreath to create a hanging loop.

HAND STITCHES

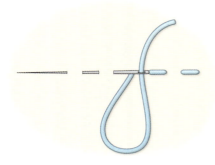

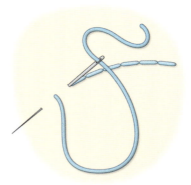

RUNNING STITCH
This is a basic stitch that has many applications. It creates a broken or dashed line, and is both functional and decorative. Simply bring the needle up and back down through the fabric, keeping the spaces between the stitches the same size as the stitches themselves.

BACKSTITCH
This stitch is both decorative and functional, and it creates a continuous line of stitches, which is perfect for seams and hems. Bring the needle up from the back, one stitch length to the left of your "start" point. Insert it one stitch length to the right and then bring it up again one stitch length in front of the point where the needle first emerged. Always work back into where the last stitch ended; this will give you a nice unbroken line.

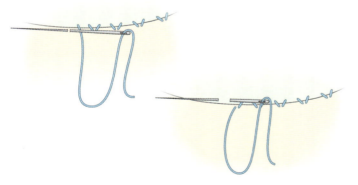

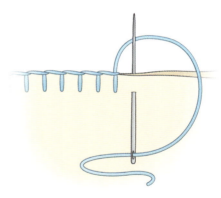

SLIPSTITCH
Slipstitch is used to close openings—for example, when you've left a gap in a seam in order to turn a piece right side out—and to appliqué one piece of fabric to another. Work from right to left. Slide the needle between the two pieces of fabric, bringing it out on the edge of the top fabric so that the knot in the thread is hidden between the two layers. Pick up one or two threads from the base fabric, then bring the needle up a short distance along, on the edge of the top fabric, and pull through. Repeat to the end.

BLANKET STITCH
This stitch is often used in appliqué and for sealing the edges of fabric. Bring the needle through at the edge of the fabric. Push the needle back through the fabric a short distance from the edge and loop the thread under the needle. Pull the thread through to make the first stitch, then make another stitch to the right of this. Continue along the fabric.

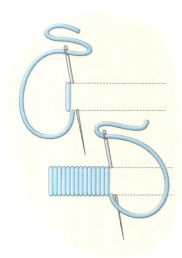
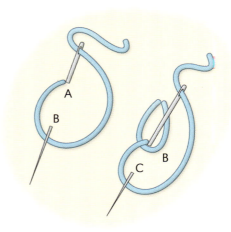

SATIN STITCH

Satin stitch is a decorative filler stitch. It consists of a series of straight stitches laid close together to completely fill a shape without any gaps.

CHAIN STITCH

Bring the needle up at A, then loop the thread and insert the needle at A again. Bring it up at B, looping the thread under the needle tip. Pull the thread through. Insert the needle at B and bring it up at C, again looping the thread under the needle tip. Continue, keeping all the stitches the same length. To anchor the last stitch in the chain, take the needle down just outside the loop, forming a little bar or "tie."

FRENCH KNOT

A purely decorative stitch and very versatile, a knot is created on the surface of your work by wrapping the thread around the needle. Bring the needle up from the back of the fabric to the front. Wrap the thread two or three times around the tip of the needle, then reinsert the needle at the point where it first emerged, holding the wrapped threads with the thumbnail of your non-stitching hand, and pull the needle all the way through.

DETACHED CHAIN STITCH

Work as for chain stitch (see above), bringing the needle up inside the loop. To finish off the stitch, take the needle down just outside the loop, forming a little bar or "tie."

HAND STITCHES 111

TEMPLATES

Most templates in this section are printed at 100%. If a template is not at 100% it will need to be enlarged, templates printed at 50% will need to be enlarged by 200%. You can do this using a photocopier.

COLLAGE CHRISTMAS CARDS AND GIFT TAGS, PAGE 10

ADVENT ENVELOPES, PAGE 22

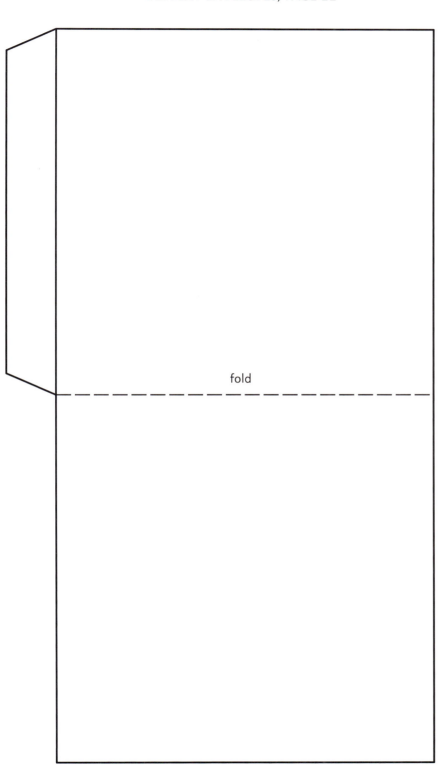

SANTA GIFT TAGS, PAGE 18

fold

MUSIC PAPER ANGELS (WINGS), PAGE 20

fold

DANISH PAPER CONES, PAGE 28

Ideas for Glitter star decorations (page 17), Glitter jars (page 25), and Star garland (page 30)

50% of actual size, enlarge by 200%

TEMPLATES 115

MITTEN GARLAND, PAGE 78

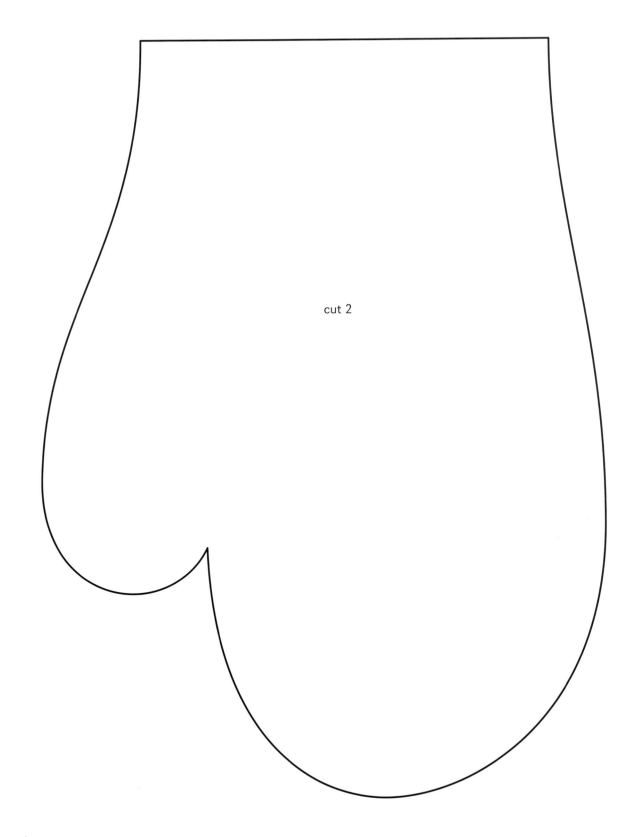

cut 2

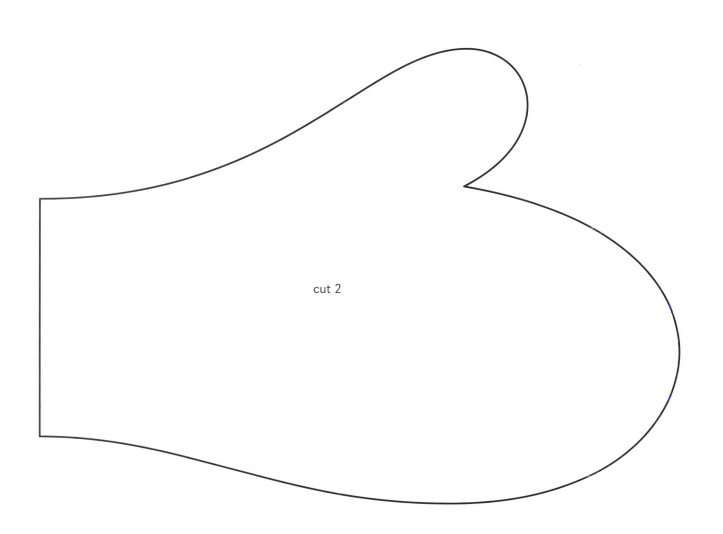

cut 2

TEMPLATES

MISTLETOE WREATH,
PAGE 70

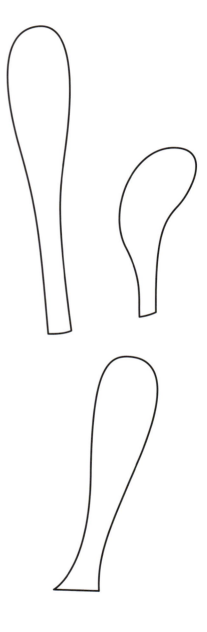

Motif ideas for Embroidered hand towels (page 82)
and Embroidered Christmas napkins (page 95)

CHRISTMAS STOCKINGS, PAGE 84

50% of actual size, enlarge by 200%

red circle: backstitch in red embroidery floss (thread)

red leaves: detached chain stitch in red embroidery floss (thread)

black dots: French knots in silver embroidery floss (thread)

red dots: French knots in red embroidery floss (thread)

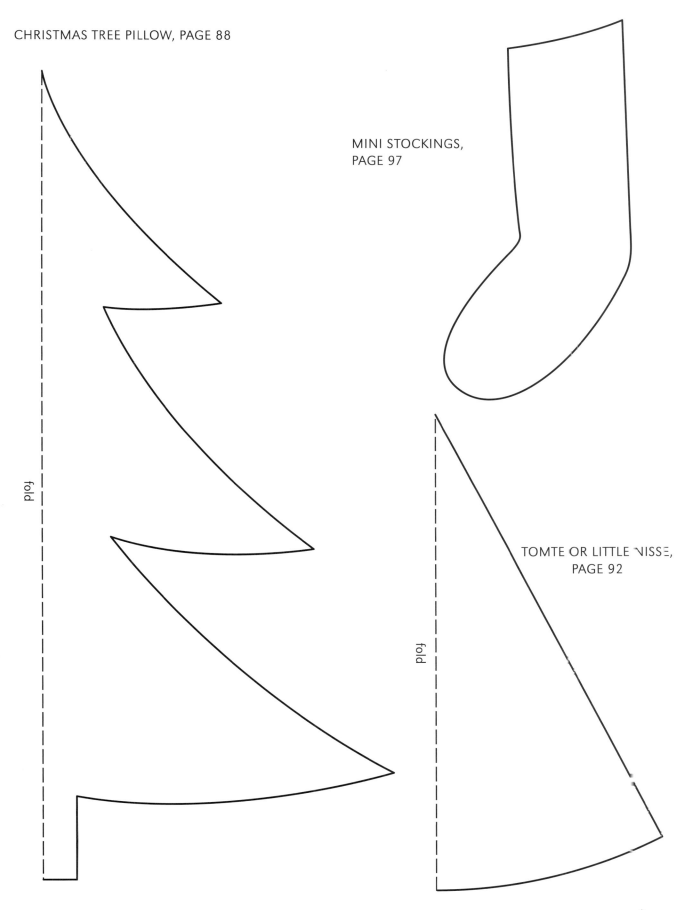

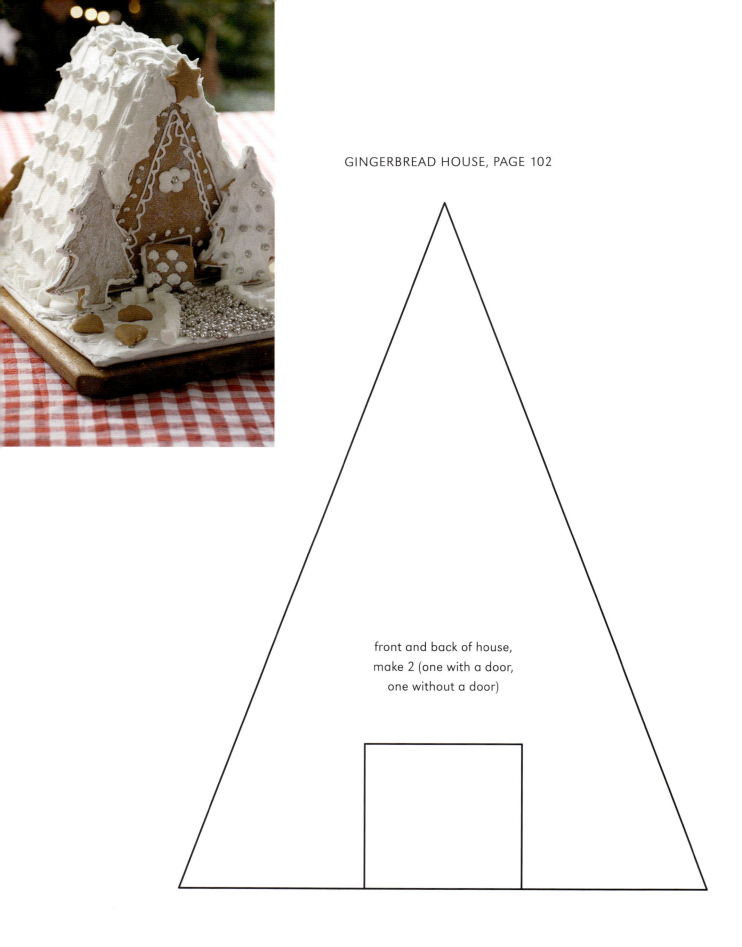

GINGERBREAD HOUSE, PAGE 102

front and back of house,
make 2 (one with a door,
one without a door)

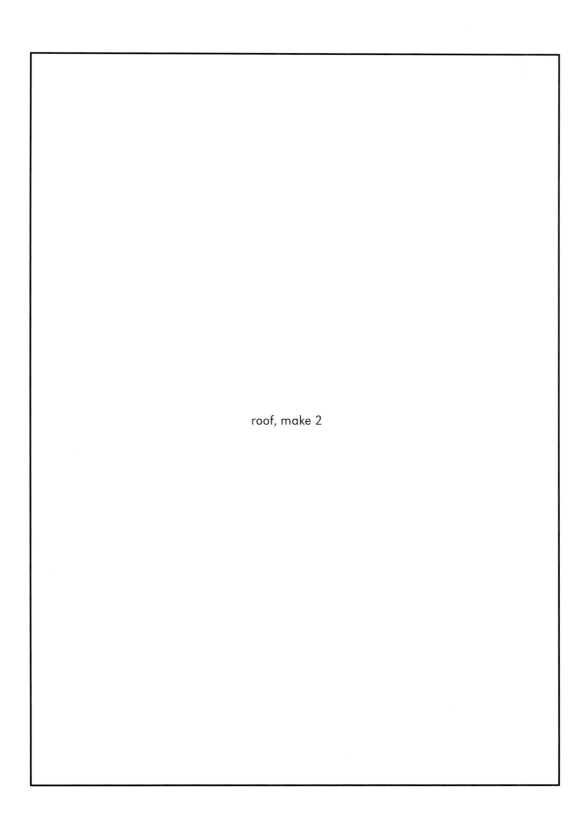
roof, make 2

RESOURCES AND SUPPLIERS

NORTH AMERICA

JOANN, www.joann.com

Michaels, www.michaels.com

Myhome Bay, Mahone Bay, Nova Scotia Canada
www.facebook.com/myhomebay

Stell's Cottage, Lunenburg, Nova Scotia, Canada
www.facebook.com/stells.cottage

UNITED KINGDOM

Country Living, www.countryliving.co.uk

The Decorative Living Fair, www.decorativelivingfair.co.uk

Hobbycraft, www.hobbycraft.co.uk

John Lewis, www.johnlewis.com

On The Green, www.onthegreenchalfont.com

Rosablue Hand-made Classics, www.rosablue.co.uk

Stable Antiques, www.stableantiques.co.uk

EUROPE

Vintage House, www.vintagehouse.dk

CHRIS'S SOCIAL MEDIA

email: chrisatthecozyclub@gmail.com

Instagram: @thecozyclubx

Facebook: The Cozy Club

YouTube: @thecozyclub4253

INDEX

Advent candle tin 41–2
Advent envelopes 22–3, 113
angels, music paper 21, 114
anise wreath 51
apple tea lights 43
apron, tea light 76–7

bag, hygge wool 80–1
baubles, patchwork quilt 63
bobbin decorations 26

candles: apple tea lights 43
　heart pillar candles 39
　little forest Advent candle tin 41–2
　tea light apron 76–7
　twig candle holders 55
　wrapped candles 13
cans, fabric-covered 61
cards, collage Christmas 10–12, 112
clothespins:
　music paper angels 21, 114
　stamped 33
clove-scented Christmas trees 73
collage Christmas cards and gift tags 10–12, 112
cones, Danish paper 28–9, 115
crab apple wreath 36

Danish paper cones 28–9, 115

embroidery: embroidered Christmas napkins 95–6, 119
　embroidered hand towels 83, 119
　little embroidered decorations 94
envelopes, Advent 22–3, 113

firelighters, pine cone 52–3
frames: framed Christmas pictures 74–5
　old window frame display 64–6

garlands: fabric garland 69
　ivy garland 54
　mitten garland 78–9, 116–17
　star garland 31, 115
gift tags: collage Christmas gift tags 10–12, 112
　Santa gift tags 18, 114
giftwrap, stamped 32
gingerbread: gingerbread hanging decorations 100–1
　gingerbread house 102–5, 122–3
　gingerbread salt dough wreath 106–7
glitter: glitter jars 25
　glitter paper trees 15–16
　glitter star decorations 17

hand towels, embroidered 83, 119
hearts: heart pillar candles 39
　heart wreath 58–60
hyacinth bulbs in a tin 38
hygge wool bag 80–1

ivy garland 54

jars: glitter jars 25
　jar covers 87

little forest Advent candle tin 41–2
Little Nisse 92–3

matchboxes, covered 67
mistletoe wreath 70–1, 118
mitten garland 78–9, 116–17

napkins, embroidered Christmas 95–6, 119

old window frame display 64–6

patchwork quilt baubles 63
pictures: framed Christmas pictures 74–5
　old window frame display 64–6
pillow, Christmas tree 88–91, 121
pine cones: pine cone family 44–6
　pine cone firelighters 52–3

salt dough wreath, gingerbread 106–7
Santa gift tags 18, 114
stamps: stamped clothespins 33
　stamped giftwrap 32
stars: glitter star decorations 17
　star garland 31, 115
stitches 108–11
stockings: Christmas stockings 84–6
　mini stockings 97, 120, 121

tea lights: apple tea lights 43
　tea light apron 76–7
templates 112–23
Tomte 92–3, 121
trees: Christmas tree pillow 88–91, 121
　clove-scented Christmas trees 73
　glitter paper trees 15–16
　twig tree 49–50
twig candle holders 55

window frame display 64–6
wool bag, hygge 80–1
wreaths: anise wreath 51
　crab apple wreath 36
　gingerbread salt dough wreath 106–7
　heart wreath 58–60
　mistletoe wreath 70–1, 118
　simple wire wreath 47

ACKNOWLEDGMENTS

I cannot thank Cindy Richards at CICO Books enough for giving me the opportunity to create my first book on Christmas in the Scandinavian style. I do not think there are enough words to express my appreciation.

Thank you to Sally Powell, Penny Craig, Kerry Lewis, Luana Gobbo, and Clare Sayer: I am grateful to you for all your efforts in helping me produce this book.

To Anna Galkina, my wonderful editor who guided me in the art of writing a book, thank you for your encouragement and patience.

Caroline Arber: your photography is simply stunning, a huge thank you, every picture captured that *hygge* feeling that I hoped to convey.

Thank you to Sophie Martell and Joanna Thornhill, my easy-going, fabulous stylists.

A huge thank you to Ben Kendrick and all at *Country Living* magazine in the UK, you helped pave the way to make all this a reality.

To all my social media followers and The Cozy Club participants—you have always believed and supported me. Thank you, it means so much.

To my mother Brigitte, I love and thank you with all my heart.

A warm and heartfelt thank you to my lovely friends and family: Kathy, Chris, Lynne, Geraldine, Laila, Felicity, Joan, Siobhan, Hester, Dawn, Ralph, Brenda, and Yvonne, you all know how I feel about your loyal and invaluable love and support throughout the years.

Finally, thank you to my lovely husband Neil "the Man in the crooked Workshop," and my sons Nicholas and Stefan. You have allowed me to create, turn the house upside down, and throw glitter everywhere! Family excursions were peppered with many stops looking for roadside treasures, antique stores, fresh flowers, and seasonal greenery. You sat waiting patiently while I hunted to my heart's content. You allowed me to fulfill my dreams, I could never have done this without the three of you. xxx